"This is a sweet and comforti
provoke your worship, and ins
you to know, love, and trust o
Tim Challies, author, *Se*

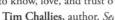

"During a difficult time in my life, the Lord used Dane Ortlund to remind me of the beautiful reality of Christ's love—that he is gentle and lowly in heart, overflowing with perfect love and compassion for sinners like me. Now, in *The Heart of Jesus*, we find these comforting gospel truths made even more accessible to needful, weary souls. I pray this book is read widely, leading many to draw near to Christ for cleansing mercy and true rest."

Scott James, author, *The Sower*; *Mission Accomplished*; *The Expected One*; and *The Risen One*

"Dane Ortlund's *The Heart of Jesus* is a profound journey into the very core of Christ's being, revealing his unfathomable love and unending compassion for humanity. Through reflections on Christ's emotions, actions, and unchanging character, Ortlund beautifully illustrates the depth of Jesus's heart, inviting readers to experience the transformative power of his love. This book not only unveils the heart of our Savior but also reassures us of his eternal devotion, making it a must-read for anyone seeking to deepen their understanding of God's boundless love."

Shane Pruitt, author, *9 Common Lies Christians Believe*; *Calling Out the Called*; and *Revival Generation*

"As a grandfather who loves to read to his grandchildren, I'm always on the lookout for good books. I look for works that will bring them joy as well as nurture their love for the Lord. I also look forward to the day when I can give them great books to read on their own. One of the first books I plan to give them is Dane Ortlund's *The Heart of Jesus*. I wouldn't be surprised if they read it over and over—just as I have read and reread Ortlund's *Gentle and Lowly*."

Randy Newman, Senior Fellow, The C. S. Lewis Institute; author, *Questioning Evangelism* and *Questioning Faith*

"During the height of the 2020 pandemic lockdown, I received a copy of Dane Ortlund's *Gentle and Lowly*. I'm not sure if there was ever a more perfect book for me, personally, at just the right time. It gave me life. I am thankful that Ortlund's scriptural thoughts on the heart of Jesus will now be accessible to those in the multigenerational church I pastor, people I desperately want to see realize the Savior's love. I believe the church will be strengthened in our affections for Christ as we grow in knowledge of his heart for us. The gospel is indeed good news. Ortlund has served us greatly by putting together this much shorter and more reader-friendly version of what I consider to be his modern classic. What a gift to be reminded of the Savior who runs to our suffering and sin rather than away from it. Take in this deep breath of fresh air."

Dean Inserra, Pastor, City Church, Tallahassee, Florida; author, *The Unsaved Christian* and *A Short Guide to Church: What Is It All About?*

"When I read *Gentle and Lowly*, it changed my life! In 47 years in church, I'd never noticed that Jesus described himself this way. It was also mind-boggling to see how Dane Ortlund described Father God as so gracious, based on Jesus's words, when I'd been taught more of the wrath and anger of God. As a public high school English teacher, I've seen how today's students have fallen behind in their reading comprehension and vocabulary acquisition, and how their attention spans have shortened. For most of them, the original version would go over their heads, or they would give up trying to read it. I am thrilled that *The Heart of Jesus* has been created, and I cannot wait to tell students and church youth groups about it!"

Jen C., mother and teacher, North Carolina

Praise for Ortlund's *Gentle and Lowly*:

"Beyond the tangible gift of this book lies the intangible gift of the gospel that *Gentle and Lowly* shares with anyone who has the privilege of reading it. Our humble fellowship has chosen to read it together so that we may all better know the 'single diamond' of Christ's heart, as conveyed in both this book and the word of God."

Thomas, inmate, San Quentin Rehabilitation Center, California

The Heart of Jesus

The Heart of Jesus

How He Really Feels about You

Dane Ortlund

:: CROSSWAY®

WHEATON, ILLINOIS

Library of Congress Cataloging-in-Publication Data

Names: Ortlund, Dane Calvin, author.
Title: The heart of Jesus : how he really feels about you / Dane C. Ortlund.
Description: Wheaton, Illinois : Crossway, 2024. | Includes bibliographical references and index.
Identifiers: LCCN 2023048462 (print) | LCCN 2023048463 (ebook) | ISBN 9781433593734 (trade paperback) | ISBN 9781433593741 (pdf) | ISBN 9781433593758 (epub)
Subjects: LCSH: Spiritual life—Christianity. | Heart—Religious aspects—Christianity. | Jesus Christ.
Classification: LCC BV4501.3 .O77 2024 (print) | LCC BV4501.3 (ebook) | DDC 232—dc23/eng/20240213
LC record available at https://lccn.loc.gov/2023048462
LC ebook record available at https://lccn.loc.gov/2023048463

Crossway is a publishing ministry of Good News Publishers.

L B		33	32	31	30	29	28	27	26	25	24
15	14	13	12	11	10	9	8	7	6	5	4	3	2	1

Affectionately dedicated, with all my heart, to my five
magnificent kids: Zach, Nate, Jer, Chloe, and Ben

"But please, please—won't you—can't you give me something that will cure Mother?"

Up till then he had been looking at the Lion's great front feet and the huge claws on them; now, in his despair, he looked up at its face. What he saw surprised him as much as anything in his whole life. For the tawny face was bent down near his own and (wonder of wonders) great shining tears stood in the Lion's eyes. They were such big, bright tears compared with Digory's own that for a moment he felt as if the Lion must really be sorrier about his Mother than he was himself.

"My son, my son," said Aslan.

C. S. LEWIS, *The Magician's Nephew*

Contents

Introduction

THIS IS A BOOK ABOUT the heart of Jesus Christ. Who is he? Who is he *really*?

What is most natural to him? What flows out most freely? Who *is* he?

In 2020 Crossway published a fuller version of the book you are now holding. It was called *Gentle and Lowly: The Heart of Christ for Sinners and Sufferers*. The purpose of this concise version of that book is to make the content more readable for a variety of other readers—young people, new believers, or anyone who would like to reflect on Christ's heart in a shorter, more accessible format. Much has been dropped and much has been lightly rewritten with these different audiences in mind. The result is this book, *The Heart of Jesus*.

Both this concise edition and the longer version have the same goal: to help Christians to see that Jesus is wonderfully different than what we think.

We tend to think that Jesus loves us when we're doing well, and puts up with us when we're not doing so well. But the Bible teaches us something different, something surprising. The love of Christ for us is just as strong when we are at our worst—and in a certain kind of way that we'll explore, his love grows even *stronger* when we are at our worst.

When we are in pain or even when we are sinning—how does Jesus feel about us? Do you ever wonder what Jesus thinks of you? The Bible answers this question with a wondrous surprise.

It is one thing to ask what Christ has done. And there are many good books on that topic of how he saves us from sin and hell. In this book, we are not focusing mainly on what Christ has done. We are considering who he is. These two matters (what he has done and who he is) are closely connected. But they are also distinct. The gospel not only gives us a clean record; it also sweeps us into Christ's very heart.

You might know that Christ died and rose again on your behalf to rinse you clean of all your sin; but do you know his deepest heart, his deepest feelings, for you? Do you live with a knowledge of what he did on the cross to forgive your sins? But do you also live with a knowledge of his longing heart for you amid your sins?

A wife may tell you many qualities about her husband—his height, his eye color, his education, his job, his friends, his hobbies, his personality, and his favorite sports team. But what can she say about his knowing gaze across the table over a dinner at their favorite restaurant? That look reflects years of their ever-deepening friendship, thousands of conversations and arguments through which they have safely come, and a settled assurance of embrace come what may. That glance speaks in a moment of his loving care more clearly than a thousand words. In short, what could she say to communicate about her husband's *heart* for her?

It is one thing to know what your husband says and does and looks like. It is something else, something deeper and more real, to know his heart for you.

So it is with Christ. It is one thing to know the truths that he is God and that he is coming back one day and a hundred other vital doctrines. It is another, deeper matter to know his heart for you.

Who is he?

1

His Very Heart

I am gentle and lowly in heart.
MATTHEW 11:29

MY DAD ONCE POINTED OUT to me something that he'd learned from the old British preacher Charles Spurgeon. In the four Gospel accounts given to us in Matthew, Mark, Luke, and John—eighty-nine chapters of the Bible—there's only one place where Jesus tells us about his own heart.

We learn much in the four Gospels about Christ's teaching. We read of his birth, his ministry, and his disciples. We are told of his travels and prayer habits. We find lengthy speeches and teachings. We learn of the way he understood himself to fulfill the whole Old Testament. And we learn in all four accounts of his unjust arrest and shameful death and astonishing resurrection.

But in only one place—perhaps the most wonderful words ever uttered by human lips—do we hear Jesus himself open up to us his very heart:

> Come to me, all who labor and are heavy laden, and I will give you rest. Take my yoke upon you, and learn from me, for *I am gentle and lowly in heart*, and you will find rest for your souls. For my yoke is easy, and my burden is light. (Matt. 11:28–30)

In the one place in the Bible where the Son of God pulls back the veil and lets us peer way down into the core of who he is, we are not told that he is "cold and demanding in heart." We are not told that he is "exalted and majestic in heart." We are not even told that he is "joyful and generous in heart." Letting Jesus set the terms, his surprising claim is that he is "gentle and lowly in heart."

One thing to get straight right from the start is that when the Bible speaks of the heart, it is not speaking simply about what we feel or our emotions. The *heart*, in Scripture, is the central reason behind all that we do. It is what gets us out of bed in the morning and what we think about as we drift off to sleep. It is our motivation headquarters. The heart, in biblical

6

terms, is not part of who we are but the center of who we are. It is what defines and directs us. The heart drives all we do.

And when Jesus tells us what animates him most deeply, what drives all he does, what we find there is: gentle and lowly.

Who could ever have thought up such a Savior?

———

"I am gentle . . ." This means that Jesus is meek. Humble. Tender. He is not trigger-happy. Not harsh, reactionary, or easily irritated.

He is the most understanding person in the universe. The posture most natural to him is not a pointed finger of accusation but open arms of embrace.

". . . and lowly . . ." The point in saying that Jesus is lowly is that he is *accessible.* For all his majestic glory and dazzling holiness, no one in human history has ever been more approachable than Jesus Christ. No admission ticket required. No hoops to jump through. The minimum bar to be welcomed into the embrace of Jesus is simply: open yourself up to him. It is all he needs. In fact, it is the only thing he works with.

Verse 28 of our passage in Matthew 11 tells us explicitly who qualifies for fellowship with Jesus: "All who labor and are heavy laden." You don't need to unburden or collect yourself and then come to Jesus. Your very burden is what qualifies you to come.

No payment is required. He says, "I will *give* you rest." His rest is a gift, not something we pull out our wallet to pay for. Jesus Christ's desire that you find rest, that you come in out of the storm, looms larger than even your own desires for such rest.

———

"Gentle and lowly." This, according to his own testimony, is Christ's very heart. This is who he is. Tender. Open. Welcoming. Accommodating. Understanding. Willing. *If we are asked to say only one thing about who Jesus is, we would be honoring Jesus's own teaching about himself if our answer is: gentle and lowly.*

If Jesus hosted his own personal website, the boldest line of the "About Me" dropdown would read: GENTLE AND LOWLY IN HEART.

Tender gentleness is who he is. It is his very heart. Jesus himself said so.

2

His Heart in Action

And he had compassion on them.

MATTHEW 14:14

WHAT WE SEE JESUS CLAIM with his words in Matthew 11:29, we see him prove with his actions time and again in all four Gospels. What he is, he does. His life proves his heart. Consider the Gospel accounts, taken as a whole:

1. When the leper says, "Lord, if you will, you can make me clean," Jesus immediately stretches out his hand and touches him, with the words, "I will; be clean" (Matt. 8:2–3). The word *will* in both the leper's request and in Jesus's answer is the Greek word for "wish" or "desire." The leper was asking about Jesus's deepest desire. And Jesus revealed his deepest desire by healing him.

2. When a group of men brings their paralyzed friend to Jesus, Jesus is so eager to help he doesn't even wait for them to speak first: "When Jesus *saw* their faith, he said to the paralytic, 'Take heart, my son; your sins are forgiven'" (Matt. 9:2). Before they could open their mouths to ask for help, Jesus couldn't stop himself—words of reassurance tumbled out.

3. Traveling from town to town, "When he saw the crowds, he had compassion for them, because they were harassed and helpless" (Matt. 9:36). So he teaches them, and he heals their diseases (9:35). Simply seeing the helplessness of the crowds, pity ignites.

4. Compassion comes in waves over and over again in Christ's ministry. His compassion drives him to heal the sick: "And he had compassion on them and healed their sick" (Matt. 14:14). It drives him to feed the hungry: "I have compassion on the crowd because they have been with me now three days and have nothing to eat" (15:32). It causes him to teach the crowds: "And he had compassion on them. . . . And he began to teach them many things" (Mark 6:34). And it brings him to wipe away the tears of those who are sad: "He had compassion on her and said

to her, 'Do not weep'" (Luke 7:13). The Greek word for "compassion" in all these texts refers to the guts of a person. It's an ancient way of referring to what rises up from deep within. This compassion reflects the deepest heart of Christ.

5. Twice in the Gospels we are told that Jesus broke down and wept. And in neither case is it sorrow for himself or his own pain. In both cases it is sorrow over another—in one case, Jerusalem (Luke 19:41), and in the other, his friend Lazarus, who has just died (John 11:35). What was his deepest anguish? The anguish of others. What drew his heart out to the point of tears? The tears of others.

6. Time and time again it is the morally disgusting, the socially hated, the disobedient, and the undeserving, who do not simply receive Christ's mercy but *to whom Christ most naturally draws near*. He is the "friend of . . . sinners" (Luke 7:34).

———

When we take the Gospels as a whole and consider the total picture given to us of who Jesus is, what stands out most strongly?

Just as dolphins can't help jumping and apple trees can't help bearing apples, what's happening inside us always shows itself through what we do. The heart reveals itself in our actions. And if the actions of Jesus reflect who he most deeply is, we cannot avoid the conclusion that it is the very fallenness, which he came to undo, that is most irresistibly attractive to him.

This is deeper than saying Jesus is loving or merciful or gracious. The testimony of the four Gospels is that when Jesus Christ sees the fallenness of the world all about him, his deepest impulse, his most natural instinct, is to move toward sin and suffering, not away from it.

Time and again in Jesus Christ's earthly ministry, his heart refused to let him sleep in. Sadness confronted him in every town. And wherever he went, whenever he was confronted with pain and longing, he embraced others with cleansing mercy.

The English preacher Thomas Goodwin said, "Christ is love covered over in flesh."[1] Picture it. If compassion clothed itself in a human body and went walking around this earth, what would it look like?

We don't have to wonder.

1 Thomas Goodwin, *The Heart of Christ* (Edinburgh: Banner of Truth, 2011), 61.

3

The Happiness of Christ

For the joy that was set before him . . .

IMAGINE THAT A COMPASSIONATE doctor has traveled deep into the jungle to provide medical care to a primitive tribe afflicted with a horrible disease. All the medical equipment has been flown in. He has correctly identified the problem, and the medicine is prepared and available. He is very wealthy and has no need to be paid anything. But as he seeks to provide care, the sick retreat back into the thickets of the jungle. They want to take care of themselves. They want to heal themselves.

Finally, a few brave young women step forward to receive the care being freely provided.

What does the doctor feel?

Joy.

His joy increases to the degree that the sick come to him for help and healing. It's the whole reason he came.

Now imagine, how much more joy he'd have if those who are sick are not strangers but his own family?

So it is with us, and so it is with Christ. He does not get flustered and frustrated when we come to him for fresh forgiveness, for renewed pardon, with distress and need and emptiness. That's the whole point. It's what he came to care for. He flew into the jungle of our world to provide healing for any who want it. He went down into the horror of death and plunged out through the other side in order to provide an endless supply of mercy and grace to his people.

When you come to Christ for mercy and love and help in your sadness and sinfulness, you are going *with* the flow of his own deepest wishes, not against them.

To put it the other way around: when we hold back, lurking in the shadows, fearful and failing, we miss out not only on our own increased comfort but on Christ's increased comfort. He lives for this. It's what he loves to do. His joy and ours rise and fall together.

THE HAPPINESS OF CHRIST

But is this way of thinking biblical?

Consider Hebrews 12. There Jesus is called "the founder and perfecter of our faith, who *for the joy that was set before him* endured the cross, despising the shame, and is seated at the right hand of the throne of God" (Heb. 12:2).

"For the joy." What joy? What was waiting for Jesus on the other side of the cross?

The joy of seeing his people enjoy what the whole book of Hebrews celebrates: cleansing forgiveness from sin. Jesus experiences joy when he sees you and me, his own brothers and sisters, receiving the medicine of his grace and love.

Perhaps it seems more natural to us to think of Jesus as receiving joy mainly when we obey him. Well, we do want to please and obey him, and surely that rejoices his heart too.

But he is thrilled also, with all his mighty heart, when we allow ourselves to truly feel forgiven. He is overjoyed as we receive his love not in a measured, restrained way, but with total freedom. Would a father with a suffocating child want his child to draw breaths from the oxygen tank in a measured, restrained way?

Remember, the Bible speaks of us as Christ's body. Christ is the head; we are his own body parts. How does a head feel about his own flesh? The apostle Paul tells us that he "nourishes and cherishes it" (Eph. 5:29). And then Paul makes the explicit connection to Christ: "Just as Christ does the church, because we are members of his body" (5:29–30). How do we care for a wounded body part? We nurse it, bandage it, protect it, and give it time to heal. For that body part isn't just a close friend; it is part of us.

That's how it is with Christ and believers. We are part of him. This is why the risen Christ asks a persecutor of his *people*, "Why are you persecuting *me*?" (Acts 9:4). When God's children hurt, Jesus himself hurts.

Jesus Christ is comforted when you draw from the riches of his atoning work because his own body is getting healed.

4

Able to Sympathize

*We do not have a high priest who is unable
to sympathize with our weaknesses.*

HEBREWS 4:15

THE PURITANS WERE A GROUP of English pastors in the
1600s. Their writing and preaching had special force because
they blended soaring theological insight with childlike hearts
of love for God. And their minds and hearts were soaked with
Scripture. A typical book written by a Puritan would take a
single verse of the Bible, wring it dry for all the comfort and
hope to be found in it, and then, several hundred pages later,
be sent off to a publisher.

One such Puritan was a man named Thomas Goodwin. In
1651 he wrote a book called *The Heart of Christ in Heaven*

towards Sinners on Earth. The single verse he was reflecting on and wringing dry was Hebrews 4:15:

> For we do not have a high priest who is unable to sympathize with our weaknesses, but one who in every respect has been tempted as we are, yet without sin.

The purpose of Goodwin's book is to help Christians of all ages who are discouraged understand something very important about Jesus. This truth is hard to believe because it is so wonderful. Goodwin's goal is to convince us that even though Jesus is now in heaven and we can't see him anymore, Jesus is just as open and tender in his embrace of sinners and sufferers as when he was on earth. In other words, Jesus is just as approachable and compassionate now, from heaven, as he ever was when he walked the earth.

———

Imagine a friend taking your hand and placing it on your father's chest to feel his beating heart. Goodwin says that Hebrews 4:15 is like that friend. This verse takes our hand and places it on Jesus Christ's own heart. He says this verse "lets us feel how his heart beats and his affections yearn toward us."[1]

1   Thomas Goodwin, *The Heart of Christ* (Edinburgh: Banner of Truth, 2011), 48.

But what exactly is Hebrews 4:15 saying? It's a deeply surprising verse. Notice the word "weaknesses": "We do not have a high priest who is unable to sympathize with our weaknesses, but one who in every respect has been tempted as we are, yet without sin." We tend to think that Jesus is with us and helping us when life is going well. That is surely true. But this text adds another truth. In a special way, it is in "our weaknesses" that Jesus sympathizes with us. In all our weakness—our fear, our anxiety, our loneliness, everything that makes us feel weak—Jesus "sympathizes" with us.

Now what does that mean? The Greek word for *sympathize* here means to "suffer with" or to "co-suffer." In other words: *When we are weak, he feels that with us.*

The theological word for this is *solidarity*, which just means "with-ness." He's right there *with* us. In our pain, Jesus is pained. In our suffering, he feels the suffering as his own even though it isn't. This doesn't mean his invincible divinity (the fact that he is God) is threatened. It means that his heart is drawn into our sadness and weakness. His love is a kind of special love that cannot be held back when he sees his people in pain.

———

But how do we know that Jesus really understands the discouragement we're facing? The text tells us: He has been "tempted" (or tested) just "as we are." Not only that, but "in every respect" as we are. The reason that Jesus is in such close solidarity with us is that the difficult path we are on is not unique to us. He has journeyed on it himself. It is not only that Jesus can relieve us from our troubles, like a doctor prescribing medicine; it is also that, before any relief comes, he is with us in our troubles, like a doctor who has endured the same disease.

Jesus is not a Marvel superhero, too strong and mighty to identify with the weak. He was a sinless man, not a sinless Superman. He woke up with bed head. He probably had pimples at thirteen. He never would have appeared on the cover of a magazine (he had "no beauty that we should desire him," Isa. 53:2). He came as a normal man to us normal men and women, boys and girls. He knows what it is to be thirsty, hungry, hated, rejected, ridiculed, excluded, embarrassed, abandoned, and misunderstood. He knows what it is to be lonely. His friends abandoned him when he needed them most; had he lived today, every last Facebook friend would have unfriended him when he turned thirty-three and was crucified.

The key to understanding the significance of Hebrews 4:15 is to push equally hard on the two phrases "in every respect" *and* "yet without sin." All our weakness—indeed, all of our life—is tainted with sin. If sin were the color blue, we do not occasionally say or do something blue; all that we say, do, and think has some taint of blue. Not so with Jesus. He had no sin. No blue at all. He was "holy, innocent, unstained, separated from sinners" (7:26). But we must ponder the phrase "in every respect" (4:15) in a way that maintains Jesus's sinlessness without diluting what that phrase means. That enticing temptation, that sore trial, that bewildering perplexity—he has been there. Indeed, because he is perfect, he has felt these pains more acutely than we sinners ever could.

———

Consider your own life.

When it feels like everyone is against you, maybe even your own parents . . . when you don't understand your feelings or emotions . . . when your best friend lets you down . . . when you feel deeply misunderstood . . . when you are laughed at . . . here is what you must know: there, right there, you have a Friend who knows exactly what such sadness feels like. He feels it himself. You belong to him. And though your friends may unfriend you, Jesus will never do that to you.

Our tendency is to feel that the more difficult life gets, the more alone we are. As we sink further into pain, we sink further into isolation. The Bible corrects us. He is *in* us, and he bears our pain with us. We are never alone. The sorrow that feels so unique to us was endured by him in the past and is now shouldered by him in the present.

If you are in Christ, you have a Friend who, in your sorrow, will never lob down a pep talk from heaven. He cannot bear to hold himself at a distance. Nothing can hold him back. His heart is too bound up with yours.

5

I Will Never Cast Out

Whoever comes to me I will never cast out.

JOHN 6:37

THE PURITAN THINKERS had lots in common with each other, but they were not all the same. Some, like Thomas Goodwin, were well educated and preached in the royal court. But others were poor and uneducated. John Bunyan was one of these.

Bunyan is most famous for writing *The Pilgrim's Progress*, a story about the Christian life, and it is, besides the Bible, history's best-selling book. But he also wrote over fifty other books. One is called *Come and Welcome to Jesus Christ*, written in 1678.

The warmth of the title reflects the tone throughout the book. In typical Puritan style, Bunyan took a single verse and wrote a whole book on it. The verse, for *Come and Welcome to Jesus Christ*, is John 6:37, where Jesus declares:

> All that the Father gives me will come to me, and whoever comes to me I will never cast out.

This was one of Bunyan's favorite verses, as evident from how often he cites it throughout his writings. But in this particular book, he takes the text and zeroes in on it, especially the second half of the verse: "Whoever comes to me I will never cast out."

At the center of his book Bunyan confronts our natural suspicions of what Jesus is like. We can easily tend to think that Jesus is welcoming to others, but not so much with us. Sure, he'll embrace others fully—but me? One by one Bunyan rejects our reasons for not coming to Jesus.

> But I am a great sinner, say you.
>
> "I will in no wise cast out," says Christ.
>
> But I am an old sinner, say you.
>
> "I will in no wise cast out," says Christ.
>
> But I am a hard-hearted sinner, say you.
>
> "I will in no wise cast out," says Christ.
>
> But I am a backsliding sinner, say you.
>
> "I will in no wise cast out," says Christ.

But I have served Satan all my days, say you.

"I will in no wise cast out," says Christ.

But I have sinned against light, say you.

"I will in no wise cast out," says Christ.

But I have sinned against mercy, say you.

"I will in no wise cast out," says Christ.

But I have no good thing to bring with me, say you.

"I will in no wise cast out," says Christ.

This promise was provided to answer all objections, and does answer them.[1]

We no longer use the expression "in no wise," but it was a seventeenth-century English way of capturing the strong language of the original Greek of John 6:37. The text literally reads, "The one coming to me I will not—*not!*—cast out." Sometimes, as here, Greek uses two negatives ("not" and "not") piled on top of each other to make the point especially strong. The idea is: "I will most certainly never, ever cast you out."

1 John Bunyan, *Come and Welcome to Jesus Christ*, in *The Works of John Bunyan*, ed. George Offor, 3 vols. (repr., Edinburgh: Banner of Truth, 1991), 1:279–80. I have lightly updated the language.

What is Jesus Christ saying to us?

Jesus's statement in John 6:37, and the book *Come and Welcome to Jesus Christ*, and the long quote above at the center of that book, all exist to calm us with the *persevering* nature of the heart of Christ.

He says, "Come to me."

We say, "But I don't deserve to . . ."

He says, "Come as you are. *I will never ever cast you out.*"

Anxious sinners like us are endless in our capacity to see reasons for Jesus to cast us out. Picture a large paper factory off the highway, with several enormous chimneys puffing out billowing smoke as the factory produces thousands of pieces of paper by the hour. We're like that factory. We constantly produce, hour by hour, reasons to believe Jesus will give up on us. We are factories of fresh resistances to Christ's love. Even when we run out of tangible reasons to be cast out, such as specific sins or failures, we tend to retain a vague sense that, given enough time, Jesus will finally grow tired of us and hold us at arm's length. Bunyan understands us. He knows we tend to deflect Christ's assurances.

"No, wait"—we say, cautiously approaching Jesus—"you don't understand. I've *really* messed up, in all kinds of ways."

I know, he responds.

"You know most of it, sure. Certainly more than what others see. But there's brokenness down inside me that is hidden from everyone."

I know it all.

"Well—the thing is, it isn't just my past. It's my present too."

I understand.

"But I don't know if I can break free of this any time soon."

That's the only kind of person I'm here to help.

"The burden is heavy—and heavier all the time."

Then let me carry it.

"It's too much to bear."

Not for me.

"You don't get it. My mistakes aren't directed toward others. They're against you."

Then I am the one most suited to forgive them.

"But the more of the ugliness in me you discover, the sooner you'll get fed up with me."

Whoever comes to me I will never cast out.

Case closed. We cannot present a reason for Jesus Christ to close off his heart to his own sheep. No such reason exists.

Every human friend has a limit. If we hurt them enough, we are cast out. The walls go up.

With Christ, though, our sins and weaknesses are the very tickets that qualify us to approach him. Nothing but coming to him is required—first at conversion, and ten thousand times throughout our present lives until we are with him in heaven.

And note that the only thing required to enjoy such love is to come to him. He does not say, "Whoever comes to me and feels *really* badly for their sin." He doesn't say, "Whoever comes to me and promises to do better next time."

He simply says, "Whoever comes to me I will never cast out."

———

As you come to him, rest in the knowledge that his grasp of you is stronger than your grasp of him. My family vacations each year in south Florida. When my two-year-old Benjamin begins to wade into the waves of the ocean, he reaches up and grabs hold of my hand. He holds on tight as the water gradually gets deeper. But a two-year-old's grip is not very strong. Before long it is not him holding on to me but me holding on to him. Left to his own strength he would certainly slip out of my hand. But if I have determined that he will not fall out of my grasp, he is secure. He can't get away from me if he tried.

So it is with Christ. We cling to him, to be sure. But our grip is that of a two-year-old amid the stormy waves of life. His sure grasp of us never falters.

Do you realize what is true of you if you are in Christ? In order for you to fall short of loving embrace into the heart of Christ, he himself would have to be pulled down out of heaven and put back in the grave. That's not going to happen. And that's how certain it is that he is never going to cast you out. He cannot bear the thought of parting with his own, even when they most deserve to be forsaken.

We say: "But I . . ."

He says: "Whoever comes to me I will never cast out."

For those united to him, Jesus is not like your teacher, who gives you good grades if you perform well enough. He is the perfect older brother, who will always stick up for you. You are not a hired worker; you are part of the family now.

His heart will never grow cold toward you, no matter how much you struggle or fail. He will never cast you out. This is who he is. This is his heart.

6

To the Uttermost

He always lives to make intercession for them.

HEBREWS 7:25

We know what he did two thousand years ago, in his life, death, and resurrection, to save us. But what about now, up in heaven? Is he twiddling his thumbs, planning his return but a little bored in the meantime?

Not at all. Jesus is engaged with his whole heart, for you, right now, even as you read this book.

And what is he doing?

The teaching of the New Testament is: He is *interceding* for his people.

The word *interceding* may be a new one for some of us. It simply means to speak on behalf of someone else. Imagine you and your family come home to a broken window in your bedroom, and your parents assume you broke it. If your brother came in and stood by you and spoke up for you, defending you, asking your father to believe your innocence, your brother would be *interceding* for you.

That's what Jesus, your older brother in God's family is doing for you every day.

How does Christ's intercession reflect his heart? Think of it this way. Christ's heart is a steady reality flowing through time. It isn't as if his heart throbbed for his people when he was on earth but has cooled off now that he is in heaven. It's not that his heart was flowing forth in a burst of mercy that took him all the way to the cross but has now grown cold. His heart is as drawn to his people now as ever it was in his incarnate state. *And the present demonstration of his heart for his people is his constant interceding on their behalf.*

———

It may be a bit confusing, however, to understand what Jesus needs to do today. Don't we speak of "the finished work of Christ upon the cross"? If he accomplished everything necessary to save us back then, what more does he need to do today?

The answer is that intercession *applies* what the atonement *accomplished.* The atonement won our salvation; intercession is the moment-by-moment application of that victory. In the past, Jesus did what he now talks about; in the present, Jesus talks about what he then did. Think of clicking the refresh button on a website. Intercession is like Jesus constantly hitting "refresh" on our innocent status in the court of heaven. The Father and the angels delight to hear hour by hour as Jesus Christ speaks on behalf of his sinning brothers and sisters on earth.

John Bunyan, the Puritan author we discussed in the last chapter, wrote a whole book on Christ's heavenly intercession called *Christ a Complete Savior.* He explains that the doctrine of intercession is a matter of Christ's heart. There's the "mathematical" side to our salvation—Jesus paid our debt and we are now free from the guilt of our sins. But there is also his interceding, which simply reflects the sheer delight Jesus has in endlessly celebrating that freedom we now enjoy. Bunyan points out that if we knew Jesus had paid our debt, but believed he was cool toward us, holding us at arm's length, we would not come to him.[1] We need to know both

1   John Bunyan, *Christ a Complete Savior*, in *The Works of John Bunyan*, ed. George Offor, 3 vols. (repr., Edinburgh: Banner of Truth, 1991), 1:221.

that he paid our debt and that he *wanted* to pay our debt. For he wanted *us*.

The key Bible passage on Christ's intercession is Hebrews 7:25:

> He is able to save to the uttermost those who draw near to God through him, since he always lives to make intercession for them.

The phrase "to the uttermost" is one Greek word (*panteles*). It means completeness, fullness, utter wholeness, like a swimming pool so full that it's overflowing.

What is the point of saying Christ saves "to the uttermost"? We who know our hearts understand. We are to-the-uttermost sinners. We need a to-the-uttermost Savior.

And that is who Jesus is.

Jesus does not take a step toward us, asking us to take a step toward him. He saves us all the way. He's a total-package Savior. Our presence in God's love and family will never sputter and die, like an engine running out of gas.

We can tend to have some small pocket of our lives, even when we're very young, where we have difficulty believing the forgiveness of God reaches. We *say* we are totally forgiven. And we really believe our sins are forgiven. Pretty much, anyway. But there's that one deep, dark part of our lives that seems so lost, so ugly, so beyond recovery. "To the uttermost" in Hebrews 7:25 means: God's forgiving, redeeming, restoring touch reaches down into those places in our lives where we are most ashamed, most defeated. More than this: those dark places are themselves where Christ loves us the most. His heart willingly goes there. His heart is *most* strongly drawn there. He knows us to the uttermost, and he saves us to the uttermost, because his heart is drawn out to us to the uttermost. We cannot sin our way out of his tender care.

———

But how do we know? The text tells us. "He is able to save to the uttermost those who draw near to God through him, *since he always lives to make intercession for them.*" Christ's heavenly intercession is the reason we know that he will save us to the uttermost.

Here's what this means. The divine Son never stops (note the word "always" in the verse) bringing his atoning life, death, and resurrection before his Father in a moment-by-moment way.

The Bible is acknowledging here that we Christians are ongoing sinners. How hopeful and realistic! Jesus continues to intercede on our behalf in heaven because we continue to fail here on earth. He does not forgive us through his work on the cross and then hope we make it the rest of the way.

Picture a glider, pulled up into the sky by an airplane, soon to be released to float down to earth. We are that glider; Christ is the plane. But he never disengages. He never lets go, wishing us well, hoping we can glide the rest of the way into heaven. He supports us all the way.

Are you a Christian? Have you acknowledged your sin, and asked Jesus to save you? If so, Jesus is interceding for you right now. The most powerful person in the universe is sticking up for you, despite the many reasons you've given him to give up on you. He will never let go. His heart won't let him.

Our sinning goes to the uttermost. But his saving goes to the uttermost. And his saving always overwhelms our sinning, because he always lives to intercede for us.

7

The Beauty of the Heart of Christ

*Whoever loves father or mother more
than me is not worthy of me.*

IN THE SUMMER OF 1740 the pastor and theologian Jonathan Edwards preached a sermon to just the children in his congregation, those ages one to fourteen. Picture the brilliant theologian, preparing a sermon in his study in Northampton, Massachusetts, considering what to say to the six- and eight- and ten-year-olds in his church. The sermon he wrote in his small, delicate handwriting covered twelve small pages. The top of the first page simply read: "To the children, Aug. 1740."[1]

What would you expect the greatest theologian in American history to say to the kids in his congregation?

Here was Jonathan Edwards's main point: "Children ought to love the Lord Jesus Christ above all things in the world."[2]

He took as his text Matthew 10:37, where Jesus says, "Whoever loves father or mother more than me is not worthy of me." It was a short sermon, taking perhaps fifteen minutes to preach. In it, Edwards lays out six reasons children should love Jesus more than anything else in life. The first is:

> There is no love so great and so wonderful as that which is in the heart of Christ. He is one that delights in mercy; he is ready to pity those that are in suffering and sorrowful circumstances; one that delights in the happiness of his creatures. The love and grace that Christ has manifested does as much exceed all that which is in this world as the sun is brighter than a candle. Parents are often full of

---

1   Jonathan Edwards, "Children Ought to Love the Lord Jesus Christ Above All," in *Sermons and Discourses 1739–1742*, ed. Harry S. Stout and Nathan O. Hatch, vol. 22 of *The Works of Jonathan Edwards* (New Haven, CT: Yale University Press, 2003), 169.

2   Edwards, "Children Ought to Love the Lord," in *Works*, 22:171.

kindness towards their children, but that is no kindness like Jesus Christ's.[3]

———

Some of you reading this book had bad parents. Maybe there's been some difficulty between you and them, even this week. Some of you had good parents, who really loved you well. Jonathan Edwards is saying: The best parent in the world does not love you anywhere close to the way Jesus loves you.

And this love of Jesus is not only great and wonderful. It is beautiful. The best love in the world is like a candle; the love of Christ for you is like the sun. It is beautiful, or lovely. Later in his sermon to the kids, he remarks:

> Everything that is lovely in God is in Christ, and everything that is or can be lovely in any man is in him: for he is man as well as God, and he is the holiest, meekest, most humble, and every way the most excellent man that ever was.[4]

What Jonathan Edwards is saying in this sermon, and what I'm trying to say in this chapter, is this: We are drawn

3 Edwards, "Children Ought to Love the Lord," in *Works*, 22:171.
4 Edwards, "Children Ought to Love the Lord," in *Works*, 22:172.

to God by the beauty of the heart of Jesus. Jesus Christ's greatness humbles us, but his heart melts us. His power makes us bow down, but his beauty makes us want to collapse into his arms.

———

Have we considered the loveliness of the heart of Christ?

Perhaps beauty is not a category that comes naturally to mind when we think about Christ. Maybe we think of him in terms of truth, not beauty. But the whole reason we care about truth and doctrine is for the sake of preserving God's beauty, just as the whole reason we care about getting the right prescription for our glasses is so that we can see clearly.

Maybe you've heard a lot about Jesus over the years, but you don't find yourself actually drawn to him. Whether you are young or old, a new believer in Jesus or someone who has believed in him for decades, what might it look like if you let Jesus draw you in through the loveliness of his heart? Allow the heart of Jesus to be something that is not only gentle toward you but lovely to you. Think about him in light of his heart. Allow yourself to be drawn to him.

Why not build in to your life times of unhurried quiet where you consider the radiance of who he actually is and what his deepest delight is? Why not give your soul room to be enchanted with Jesus Christ time and again?

When you look at the glorious older Christians in your church, how do you suppose they got there? Sound doctrine, yes. Resolute obedience to God, without a doubt. Suffering without grumbling, for sure.

But maybe another reason, maybe the deepest reason, is that they have, over time, been won over in their deepest affections to a beautifully tender Savior. Perhaps they have simply tasted, over many years, the surprise of a Christ for whom their very sins draw him in rather than push him away. Maybe they have not only known that Jesus loved them but felt it.

———

We can't close this chapter without thinking about the children in our lives. Perhaps some of you who are reading this book are yourselves quite young. If you've made it this far—well done!

Jonathan Edwards told the kids he knew, "There is no love so great and so wonderful as that which is in the heart of Christ." How might we, in our own way and time, communicate this love to the kids all around us?

What is it that the children whom we greet in the hallways of our churches need? Most deeply? Yes, they need friends, and encouragement, and help with homework, and three meals a day. But their deepest need, the thing that will sustain them when all these other needs go unmet, is sensing the heart-melting beauty of who Jesus is for them. How he actually feels about them, no matter how well they are doing in life and school and friendships.

If you're a young person growing up in a Christian family, or perhaps a college student who has recently become a Christian, the most important thing for you to know is the tender beauty of the heart of Jesus Christ for you in your ups *and your downs*. He loves you with all his mighty heart.

If you're a parent of children, the most important thing for you to do for your kids is to show them that even the best love of a mother or father is a shadow of a greater love from Christ. Our goal is to make the tender heart of Christ irresistible and unforgettable to our children. Our central goal is that our kids would leave the house at eighteen and be unable to live the rest of their lives believing that their sins and sufferings repel Christ.

That Jesus is gentle and lowly in heart is not only true. It is also beautiful. Let his tender beauty draw you into his arms this very day—not once you get better at following him, but now, right now.

8

The Emotional Life of Christ

When Jesus saw her weeping . . . he was deeply
moved in his spirit and greatly troubled.

JOHN 11:33

WHATEVER IT MEANS to be human, Jesus was and is. He had no sin; but in every other way, he was a true human being.

He had fingerprints. His eyes were a certain color. He trimmed his toenails and cleaned his teeth. He got tired and slept. He cried at times.

And there is one particular fact of being a human that he also experienced, though we don't talk about it much: he had emotions.

Our emotions are infected with sin, of course. But emotions are not themselves a result of the fall. Jesus experienced the full range of emotions that we do (Heb. 2:17; 4:15).[1]

A great theologian, B. B. Warfield (1851–1921), wrote a famous essay in 1912 called "On the Emotional Life of Our Lord." In it he explored what the Bible shows us about Christ's emotions. In other words, what do we learn from Matthew, Mark, Luke, and John about what Jesus felt on the inside?

———

Warfield begins his study of specific emotions in the life of Christ by noting that when we read the four Gospels carefully, the most common emotion in the life of Jesus is compassion.[2] He gives various examples, while all the time trying to help us see that Jesus was not only compassionate in his actions, but that he actually felt inner turmoil and pity toward the unfortunate. When the blind and the lame and the sad appealed to Jesus, "his heart responded with a profound feeling of pity for them."[3]

Hearing the plea, for example, of two blind men begging for sight (Matt. 20:30–34) or that of the leper begging

---

1   B. B. Warfield, *The Person and Work of Christ* (Oxford, UK: Benediction Classics, 2015), 137–38.

2   Warfield, *The Person and Work of Christ*, 96.

3   Warfield, *The Person and Work of Christ*, 97–98.

for cleansing (Mark 1:40–41), or simply seeing a distressed woman (Luke 7:12–13), "set our Lord's heart throbbing with pity."[4]

Perhaps some of us think that because Jesus was God, emotions (such as compassion) would not be felt as strongly. But Jesus was not half God, half man. He was fully God and fully man. And as fully man, he experienced all emotion without sin.

And here's the key point: the fact that he was a perfect man means that he experienced compassion *all the more*.

Perhaps an example would clarify. I remember walking the streets of a large city in India several years ago. I had just finished preaching at a church and was waiting for my ride to arrive. Immediately outside the church grounds was an older man, homeless, sitting in a cardboard box. His clothes were torn and dirty. He was missing several teeth. And what was immediately most alarming was his hands. Most of his fingers were partly missing. It was clear they had not been damaged by an injury but had simply been eaten away over time. He was a leper.

What happened in my heart in that moment? My fallen, sinful heart? Compassion. A little, anyway. But it was shallow

4 Warfield, *The Person and Work of Christ*, 98.

45

compassion. The fall has ruined me, all of me, including my emotions. Fallen emotions not only sinfully overreact; they also sinfully underreact. Why was my pity so small toward this miserable man? Because I am a sinner.

What then must it mean for a sinless man, with perfect emotions, to lay eyes on that leper?

What would unrestrained emotions of compassion be like?

It would be an overflowing compassion.

That is what Jesus felt when he looked on men and women, boys and girls, who were sad or in pain. Perfect, unfiltered compassion.

And it is what he feels as he looks at you in your sadness and pain.

He feels it more deeply than you do.

9

A Tender Friend

. . . a friend of tax collectors and sinners!

MATTHEW 11:19

ONE CATEGORY IN WHICH to think about the heart of Christ is that of friendship. His heart binds him to us as our never-failing friend.

What kind of person does Jesus enjoy befriending? We find out when we hear his enemies making fun of him. They ridicule him as "a friend of tax collectors and sinners!"—that is, a friend of the most horrible kinds of people we can think of (Matt. 11:19).

The crowds call him this as an accusation. But for those of us who know ourselves to be sinners, the label "friend of sinners" is a deep comfort.

What does it mean that Christ is a friend to sinners? At the very least, it means that he enjoys spending time with them. It also means that they feel welcome and comfortable around him. Notice the passing line that starts off a series of parables in Luke: "Now the tax collectors and sinners were all drawing near to hear him" (Luke 15:1). The very two groups of people whom Jesus is accused of befriending in Matthew 11 are those who can't stay away from him in Luke 15. They are at ease around him. They sense something different about him. Others avoid them. But Jesus offers them the surprise of welcome. Of friendship.

What he is really doing, at bottom, is pulling them into his heart.

———

Consider your own relationships.

The line of who your friends are could be drawn in varying places, like circles getting smaller and smaller on a dartboard, narrowing in to a bull's-eye. There are some people in our lives whose names we know, but they're not friends. Others are closer to the middle; we hang out sometimes, and we like them, but we don't have deep affection for them. Continuing to move toward the center, some of us are blessed to have a particularly close friend or two, someone who really knows us and "gets" us. It might be a husband or wife who is our closest earthly friend. If you're too young to be married, maybe you have a best friend, someone you just love being with every chance you get.

Even walking through this brief thought experiment, of course, is painful for many of us. We realize that we do not have one true friend, someone we could go to with any problem knowing we would not be turned away. Who in our lives do we feel safe with—really safe, safe enough to open up about *anything*? For many of us, the answer, sadly, is no one.

Here is the promise of the gospel and the message of the whole Bible: *In Jesus Christ, we are given a friend who will always enjoy rather than refuse our presence.*

This is a companion whose embrace of us does not strengthen or weaken depending on how clean or unclean, how attractive or ugly, how obedient or disobedient, we presently are.

Won't most of us admit that even with our best friends, we don't feel fully comfortable divulging *everything* about our lives? We like them, and even love them, and go on vacation with them, and sing their praises to others—but we don't really, at the deepest heart level, *entrust* ourselves to them.

But what if you had a friend at the center of the bull's-eye of your relationship circle, whom you knew would never raise his eyebrows at what you shared with him? Even the worst parts of you?

All our human friendships have a limit to what they can handle. But what if there were a friend with no limit? No ceiling on what he would put up with and still want to be with you?

Consider Jesus in Revelation 3. There he says to a group of Christians who are "wretched, pitiable, poor, blind, and naked" (3:17): "Behold, I stand at the door and knock. If anyone hears my voice and opens the door"—what will Jesus do?—"I will come in to him and eat with him, and he with me" (3:20).

Jesus wants to be with you. He wants to come in to you—wretched, pitiable, poor you—and enjoy meals together. Spend time with you. Deepen the relationship. *He enjoys your presence, as you are.*

———

We should not overly domesticate Jesus here. He is not just any friend. A few chapters earlier in Revelation we see a portrayal of Christ so overwhelming to John that he falls down, unable to move (1:12–17). He is a majestic Lord.

But we need to draw strength and comfort from his posture in Revelation 3 and see his desire to spend time with us. He isn't waiting for you to trigger his heart. He is already standing at the door, knocking, wanting to come in to you.

What's our job?

It is to let him in. Let him be that friend you deeply desire.

Jesus tells us, "You are my friends" (John 15:15). We did not fill out a "friendship with Jesus" application, and now await his answer. He himself created the friendship. He is walking with us through our difficult lives.

Jonathan Edwards preached that the whole reason Jesus came down from heaven and walked this earth was "that he might be near to you and might be your companion."[1] *Companion* is another word for friend, but it specifically speaks of the idea of someone who goes with you on a journey. As we make our pilgrimage through this wide wilderness of a world, we have a steady, constant companion.

Jesus Christ's heart for us means that he will be our never-failing friend no matter what friends we do or do not enjoy on earth. He offers us a friendship that gets underneath the pain of our loneliness. While that pain

1 Jonathan Edwards, "The Spirit of the True Saints Is a Spirit of Divine Love," in *The Glory and Honor of God: Volume 2 of the Previously Unpublished Sermons of Jonathan Edwards*, ed. Michael McMullen (Nashville, TN: Broadman, 2004), 339.

does not go away, we can still rejoice our way through our loneliness, because we have Jesus. He walks with us through every moment.

He knows the pain of being betrayed by a friend, but he will never betray us. He will not even so much as *coolly* welcome us. That is not who he is. That is not his heart.

10

Why the Spirit?

I will ask the Father, and he will
give you another Helper.

JOHN 14:16

THIS IS A BOOK ABOUT JESUS CHRIST, the Son, the second person of the Trinity. But how does the gentle and lowly heart of Jesus Christ relate to the other two persons of the Trinity, the Spirit and the Father?

We will give a chapter to each, asking what the Bible teaches about how the heart of Christ relates to the Spirit and then to the Father.

First, the Spirit. What is the role of the Holy Spirit? What does he actually do? There are many valid biblical answers to that question. The Spirit . . .

- gives us new birth (John 3:6–7)
- empowers us with gifts (1 Cor. 12:4–7)
- assures us that we are God's children (Gal. 4:6)
- leads us (Gal. 5:18, 25)
- makes us fruitful (Gal. 5:22–23)
- enables us to kill sin (Rom. 8:13)
- guides us into truth (John 16:13)
- transforms us into the image of Christ (2 Cor. 3:18)

These are all gloriously true. In this chapter I'd like to add just one more action to this list: *The Spirit causes us to actually feel Christ's heart for us.*

———

Think of the difference between reading a book about the beach of Jamaica and actually traveling there to enjoy it. The book is good and true; but it does not give you the experience. You don't feel the sun on your face and the sand between your toes and the cool refreshing water as you wade.

In a similar way, if there were no Holy Spirit, all we would ever be doing would be reading about Christ's heart (as you are in this book). The Holy Spirit moves you from the book to the experience. From idea to reality. From hearing to seeing.

It's like what happened to Job at the very end of the book of Job when he says to God:

> I had heard of you by the hearing of the ear,
>   but now my eye sees you. (Job 42:5)

That's what the Holy Spirit does.

It is one thing, as a child, to be told your father loves you. You believe him. You take him at his word. But it is another thing, far more real, to be swept up in his embrace. To feel the warmth, to hear his beating heart within his chest, to instantly know how safe you are in the strong grip of his arms.

———

In John 14–16 Jesus explains the work of the Spirit as the continuing of his own work:

> But now I am going to him who sent me, and none of you asks me, "Where are you going?" But because I have said these things to you, sorrow has filled your heart. Nevertheless, I tell you the truth: it is to your advantage that I go away, for if I do not go away, the Helper will not come to you. But if I go, I will send him to you. (John 16:5–7)

Jesus is leaving. And so the disciples are sad. Sorrow has filled their hearts.

But Jesus says it is to the disciples' advantage that he is going away. So apparently it is even better to have the Spirit within them.

Consider what this means. Jesus had befriended them and embraced them into his heart, so they thought that Jesus leaving meant Jesus's heart leaving. But *the Spirit is the answer to how Jesus can leave them bodily while leaving his heart behind.*

The Holy Spirit is the continuation of the heart of Christ for his people after the departure of Jesus to heaven. As the Puritan Thomas Goodwin says, the Spirit "shall be a better Comforter to you than I am to be. . . . He will comfort you better than I should do with my bodily presence." The Spirit will tell believers "nothing but stories of my love."[1] Goodwin then makes the connection to Christ's heart: "So that you shall have my heart as surely and as speedily as if I were with you; and he will be continually breaking your hearts, either with my love to you, or yours to me, or both."[2]

Jesus said that he is "gentle and lowly in heart" (Matt. 11:29). That is a beautiful statement, and even without the

1   Thomas Goodwin, *The Heart of Christ* (Edinburgh: Banner of Truth, 2011), 18–19. I have lightly updated the language.

2   Goodwin, *The Heart of Christ*, 19–20.

Spirit one could respect and even marvel at it. But the Spirit takes those words of Christ's and sets them aglow within us. The Spirit turns the recipe into actual taste.

This is why Paul says that believers are given "the Spirit who is from God, that we might understand the things freely given us by God" (1 Cor. 2:12). When Paul says *understand* he does not merely mean to "understand" that two plus two equals four. It is a deeper, felt understanding, the way you understand that chocolate is sweet when you place it in your mouth. Paul is saying that the Spirit has been given to us in order that we might know, way down deep, the endless grace of the heart of God. "Freely given" in this text is simply the verb form (*charizomai*) of the common Greek word for "grace" (*charis*). In other words, we could translate 1 Corinthians 2:12 like this: "The Spirit who is from God, that we might understand God's deep grace." The Spirit loves nothing more than to awaken and calm and soothe us with the knowledge of what we have been graced with.

The Spirit's role, in summary, is to turn our postcard-like knowledge of Christ's great heart of longing affection for us into an experience of sitting on the beach, in a lawn chair, drink in hand, enjoying the actual experience. The Spirit does this decisively, once and for all, when we become Christians through new birth. But he does it ten thousand times thereafter, as we continue through sin, pain, or boredom to drift from the felt experience of Jesus Christ's heart.

11

Father of Mercies

. . . the Father of mercies and God of all comfort.

2 CORINTHIANS 1:3

"WHAT COMES INTO OUR MINDS when we think about God is the most important thing about us." So begins A. W. Tozer's book *The Knowledge of the Holy*.[1] And the whole point of what I'm writing in this book of Christ's heart is to clarify what God is actually like, instead of what we expect him to be like. I am trying to help us leave behind our natural, fallen intuitions that God is distant and cold and to step into the freeing knowledge that he is gentle and lowly in heart.

1   A. W. Tozer, *The Knowledge of the Holy* (New York: HarperCollins, 1961), 1.

But our study focuses on the Son of God. What about God the Father?

Should the Son as gentle and lowly be "what comes into our minds" but should we think of the Father as something else? Is the Father a little less gentle, maybe?

This chapter answers that question.

———

There seems to be a common idea among Christians that the Son is the nicest member of the Trinity. The Father loves us too, of course. But he's a little colder. More stern. The Son is the *really* loving one.

But this is not what the Bible teaches. It is true that the Father's wrath was satisfied by the Son's work on the cross. But the Father's heart is just as filled up with love for you as the Son's. The Son's work on the cross opened the way for the Father's love to flow down to us, but it did not increase the Father's love for us.

The Bible is clear that the Father's heart is just as full of love for his people as the Son's heart. In 2 Corinthians 1:3, for example, we read:

Blessed be the God and Father of our Lord Jesus Christ, the Father of mercies and God of all comfort.

"The Father of mercies." As Paul opens 2 Corinthians he gives us a window into what came into *his* mind when he thought about God.

Yes, the Father is just and righteous. Perfectly so. Without such a truth, we would have no hope that all wrongs would one day be put right.

But what is his heart?

What flows out from his deepest being?

Mercies.

He is "the Father of mercies." Just as a father has children who reflect who he is, the divine Father has mercies that reflect him. There is a family resemblance between the Father and mercy.

To speak of God the Father as the Father of mercies is to say that he multiplies compassionate mercies to his needful, wayward, messy, fallen, wandering people. This is the Bible's way of taking us into who God the Father is. A correct understanding of the triune God is not that of a Father whose central disposition is judgment and a Son whose central disposition is love. The heart of both is one and the same; this is, after all, one God, not two. Theirs is a heart of redeeming love. This is not a love that softens his justice and wrath but a love that beautifully satisfies his justice and wrath.

What should come into our minds when we think about God? The triune God is three in one, a fountain of endless mercies. These mercies flow down to us and abundantly provide for us in all of our many needs and failures and wanderings. This is who he is. Father no less than Son, and Son no less than Father.

Beyond what we are aware of at any given moment, the Father's tender care envelopes us with pursuing gentleness, sweetly governing every last detail of our lives. He orders the flutter of the leaf that falls from the tree and the breeze that knocked it free (Matt. 10:29–31), and he controls the bomb that evil minds detonate (Amos 3:6; Luke 13:1–5). But through and underneath and fueling all that washes into our lives, great and small, is the heart of a Father. The Father of mercies.

Some of us had great dads growing up. Others of us were horribly mistreated by them. Whatever the case, the good in our earthly dads is a faint pointer to the true goodness of our heavenly Father, and the bad in our earthly dads is the opposite of who our heavenly Father is. He is the Father of whom every human father is a shadow.

———

In John 14, Philip asks Jesus to show the disciples the Father (14:8). Jesus responds: "Have I been with you so long, and you still do not know me, Philip? Whoever has seen me has seen the Father" (14:9).

"Whoever has seen me has seen the Father."

Jesus Christ is the visible manifestation of the invisible God (2 Cor. 4:4, 6; Heb. 1:3). In him we see heaven's heart walking around on two legs in time and space. When we see the heart of Christ throughout the four Gospels, we are seeing the very compassion and tenderness of who God himself most deeply is.

As you consider the Father's heart for your own life, let him be the Father of mercies *to you*. He is not cautious in his tenderness toward you. He multiplies mercies for your every need, and there is nothing he would rather do. "Remember," said the Puritan John Flavel, "that this God is your Father, and is more tender toward you than you are, or can be, toward yourself."[2] In other words, your gentlest treatment of yourself is not as gentle as the way your heavenly Father handles you.

The heart of Christ is gentle and lowly. And that is the perfect picture of who the Father is. "The Father himself loves you" (John 16:27).

---

2   John Flavel, *Keeping the Heart: How to Maintain Your Love for God* (Fearn, UK: Christian Heritage, 2012), 57. I have slightly updated the language.

12

The Lord, the Lord

"A God merciful and gracious, slow to anger . . ."

WHAT DO YOU THINK OF when you hear the phrase "the glory of God"? Do you picture the immense size of the universe? A thundering, terrifying voice from the clouds?

In Exodus 33 Moses asks God, "Please show me your glory" (33:18).

How does God respond?

"I will make all my goodness pass before you" (33:19).

Goodness? Isn't the glory of God a matter of his greatness, not his goodness? Might, not mercy?

Apparently not. God then goes on to speak of showing grace and mercy to whomever he wills (33:19). He then tells Moses that he will place him in a cleft of the rock and that (once again) his *glory* will pass by (33:22). And the Lord does pass by and yet (once again) defines his glory in 34:6–7 as a matter of mercy and grace:

> . . . merciful and gracious, slow to anger, and abounding in steadfast love and faithfulness, keeping steadfast love for thousands, forgiving iniquity and transgression and sin, but who will by no means clear the guilty, visiting the iniquity of the fathers on the children and the children's children, to the third and the fourth generation.

When we speak of God's glory, we are speaking of who God is, what he is like, his distinctive radiance, what makes God *God*.

And when God himself sets the terms on what his glory is, he surprises us into wonder. We expect him to be thundering, judging, condemning. After all, we each have so much sin in our lives. And then Exodus 34 taps us on the shoulder and stops us in our tracks. The desire of God's heart is mercy. His glory is his goodness. His glory is his lowliness. As David said:

> Great is the glory of the LORD.
> For though the LORD is high, he regards the lowly.
>   (Ps. 138:5–6)

Consider the actual words of Exodus 34:6–7.

"Merciful and gracious." These are the first words out of God's own mouth after proclaiming his name ("the LORD," or "I AM"). *The first words.* The only two words Jesus will use to describe his own heart are *gentle* and *lowly* (Matt. 11:29). And the first two words God uses to describe who he is are *merciful* and *gracious* (Ex. 34:6). God does not reveal his glory as, "The LORD, the LORD, disappointed and frustrated." His highest priority and deepest delight and first reaction—his heart—is merciful and gracious. He gently accommodates himself to our terms rather than overwhelming us with his.

"Slow to anger." He doesn't have his finger on the trigger. It takes a long time to get him angry. Unlike us, who are often emotional dams ready to break, God can put up with a lot. This is why the Old Testament speaks of God being "provoked to anger" by his people dozens of times. But not once are we told that God is "provoked to love" or "provoked to mercy." His anger requires provocation; his mercy is pent up, ready to gush forth. We tend to think that divine anger is pent up, spring-loaded; while divine mercy is slow to build. But it's just the opposite. Divine mercy is ready to burst forth at the slightest prick.

"Abounding in steadfast love and faithfulness." There is one Hebrew word underlying the English phrase "steadfast love."

It is the word *hesed*. This is God's special commitment to his people, because he has gladly bound himself to them in an unbreakable bond. The word "faithfulness" further clarifies this commitment—he will never throw his hands up in the air, despite all the reasons his people give him to do so. He refuses even to entertain the notion of withdrawing his heart from us the way we pull back from others who hurt us. And so he is not simply *existing* in large-hearted covenant commitment but *abounding* in it. His determined commitment to us never runs dry.

"Keeping steadfast love for thousands" (Ex. 34:7). This could equally be translated "keeping steadfast love to a thousand generations," as we read in Deuteronomy 7:9: "The LORD your God is God, the faithful God who keeps covenant and steadfast love with those who love him and keep his commandments, *to a thousand generations*." This does not mean that his goodness shuts off with generation number 1,001. It is God's own way of saying: *There is no end to my commitment to you. You can't outrun my mercy. You can't escape my goodness. My heart is set on you.*

"Visiting the iniquity of the fathers on the children and the children's children, to the third and the fourth generation" (Ex. 34:7). These closing words are hard to hear at first, but they actually foster further comfort. God is assuring us he is not a softie. He is the one perfectly fair person in the universe. Sin and guilt pass down from generation to generation. But notice what God says. While family sins trickle down to the third or fourth generation, his covenant love flows down to a thousand generations. Do you see the difference? Yes, our sins will be passed down to our children and grandchildren. But God's goodness will be passed down in a way that swallows up all our sins. His mercies travel down a thousand generations, far eclipsing the third or fourth generation.

———

That is who God is. That, according to his own testimony, is his heart.

The Christian life is the long journey of letting our natural thoughts about who God is, over many years, fall away. We must allow our thoughts to be replaced with God's own insistence on who he is.

This is hard work. It takes a lot of time and a lot of suffering to believe that God's deepest heart is "merciful and gracious, slow to anger" (Ex. 34:6). Perhaps Satan's greatest victory in your life today is not the sin in which you regularly indulge. Perhaps the devil's greatest victory in your life is the dark thoughts you hold about God's heart that cause you to not go to him in the first place and keep you cool toward him in the wake of sinning.

But of course the final proof of who God is cannot be found in Exodus but in Matthew, Mark, Luke, and John. In Exodus 33–34, Moses cannot see God's face and live, because it would destroy him. But what if one day humans did see the face of God in a way that did not destroy them?

The Lord passed by Moses and said that his deepest glory is seen in his mercy and grace. Jesus came to do in flesh and blood what God had done only in wind and voice in the Old Testament.

When we see the Lord revealing his truest character to Moses in Exodus 34, we are seeing the shadow that will one day yield to the shadow caster, Jesus Christ, in the Gospels.

We hear about God's deepest heart in Exodus 34. But we see that heart in the Galilean carpenter.

13

His Ways Are Not Our Ways

My thoughts are not your thoughts.

ISAIAH 55:8

THE MESSAGE OF THIS BOOK is that we tend to project our natural expectations about who God is onto him instead of letting the Bible surprise us into what God himself says. Nowhere in the Bible is that point made more clearly than in Isaiah 55.

When life takes a difficult turn, Christians often remind others, with a shrug, "His ways are not our ways!" In other words, God works in ways we don't understand.

That is certainly true. Much of what God does, and why, is a mystery to us. But the passage in which we find "his ways are not our ways" comes from Isaiah 55:8. And in context, it means something quite different. It is a statement not of the surprise of God's mysterious working but of the surprise of God's compassionate heart. The full passage goes like this:

Seek the LORD while he may be found;
    call upon him while he is near;
let the wicked forsake his way,
    and the unrighteous man his thoughts;
let him return to the LORD, that he may have
        compassion on him,
    and to our God, for he will abundantly pardon.
For my thoughts are not your thoughts,
    neither are your ways my ways, declares the LORD.
For as the heavens are higher than the earth,
    so are my ways higher than your ways
    and my thoughts than your thoughts.
        (Isa. 55:6–9)

Notice exactly how God is reasoning here.

He calls us to seek him, to call on him, and invites even the wicked to return to the Lord. What will happen when we do this? God will "have compassion on" us (55:7). How exactly will God have compassion on us? The text goes on: "He will abundantly pardon" (55:7). In other words, he will forgive us lots, not a little. He'll forgive ("pardon") everything bad we ever do. This is deep comfort for us as we find ourselves time and again wandering away from the Father, looking for soul calm anywhere but in his love. Whenever we return to God, however ashamed and disgusted we are with ourselves, he will abundantly pardon us. He does not merely accept us. He sweeps us up in his arms again.

———

But notice what the text then does. Verses 8 and 9 take us deeper into this compassion and abundant pardon. Verse 7 has told us what God does; verses 8 and 9 tell us who he is. Or to put it differently, God knows that *even when we hear of his compassionate pardon, we latch on to that promise with a diminished view of the heart from which that compassionate pardon flows.* This is why the Lord continues:

> For my thoughts are not your thoughts,
> neither are your ways my ways, declares the LORD.
> For as the heavens are higher than the earth,
> so are my ways higher than your ways
> and my thoughts than your thoughts. (55:8–9)

What is God saying? He is telling us that we cannot view his expressions of his mercy with our old eyes. Our very view of God must change.

What would we say to a six-year-old who, upon being given a birthday gift by his loving father, immediately scrambled to reach for his piggy bank to try to pay his dad back? How painful to a father's heart! That little child does not yet understand what his father delights to do.

The deep belief of our fallen hearts is that God treats us according to what we deserve. Because we are sinful, we do not view God accurately. Our capacity to see clearly the heart of God has gone into meltdown. We are left with a diseased view of how he feels about his people, without even realizing what we're doing. We're like a grandson who, given a crisp one-hundred-dollar bill, concludes that his grandfather must be very wealthy, not knowing the billions in real estate of which that gift is just the tiniest reflection.

So God tells us in plain terms how tiny our natural views of his heart are. His thoughts are not our thoughts. His ways are not our ways. And not because we're just a few degrees off. No, "as the heavens are higher than the earth"—that's a long way—"so are my ways higher than your ways and my thoughts than your thoughts" (55:9).

In verse 8 God says his *ways* and ours are different; in verse 9 he gets more specific and says his *thoughts* are higher. God's very thoughts—his plans, his purposes, his way of approaching us—are higher, grander, enveloped in a compassion for which we fallen sinners have no natural category.

To speak of God's "ways" and "thoughts" is very close to speaking of his heart. All this language (ways, thoughts, heart) is getting at who he most deeply is: the spring-loaded tilt of his affections, what he delights in most. And according to Isaiah 55, it is the opposite of what we expect.

———

In other words: God isn't like you. Even the most intense of human love is only a faint echo of heaven's flood-like forgiveness. His heartful thoughts for you outstrip what you can imagine. He intends to restore you into the bright glory for which you were created. And that is dependent not on you keeping yourself clean but on you taking your mess to him. He doesn't limit himself to working with the unspoiled parts of us that remain after a lifetime of sinning. His power runs so deep that he is able to redeem the ugliest parts of our past into the most beautiful parts of our future.

All he asks is that you humble yourself enough to fall into his open arms, arms that abundantly pardon.

It is what he does. It is who he is.

His ways are not our ways.

14

Yearning for You

My heart yearns for him.

JEREMIAH 31:20

THE HIGH POINT of the book of Jeremiah is chapters 30–33. Bible teachers call these chapters the "Book of Consolation." *Consolation* means comfort—it's what you feel when you're five years old and your dad or mom gives you a big hug after you've fallen off your bike. And here in the middle of Jeremiah, God reveals to his people his final response to their selfishness. And it is not what they deserve. Though they expect judgment, he surprises them with comfort. Why? Because he had pulled them into his heart, and they cannot sin their way out of it. "I have loved you with an everlasting love," he assures them (Jer. 31:3).

Well of course! We might be thinking. *Israel is God's people. He's supposed to love them.*

But do we realize what has been happening in the first twenty-nine chapters of Jeremiah? To take just a single sentence from each of the opening chapters:

- "I will declare my judgments against them, for all their evil" (1:16).
- "My people . . . have forsaken me" (2:13).
- "You have polluted the land with your vile whoredom" (3:2).
- "O Jerusalem, . . . how long shall your wicked thoughts lodge within you?" (4:14).
- "This people has a stubborn and rebellious heart" (5:23).

And so on, through twenty-nine chapters. And then, on the other side of chapters 30–33, the rest of the book is judgment against the nations (Jeremiah 34–52).

But here at the center of Jeremiah is the Book of Consolation. And within these four chapters, the text that sums it all up best is 31:20:

Is Ephraim my dear son?
　Is he my darling child?

For as often as I speak against him,
    I do remember him still.
Therefore my heart yearns for him;
    I will surely have mercy on him,
                   declares the LORD.

"Ephraim" is just another term for Israel, God's people, though it appears to be a sort of divine term of affection for Israel throughout the Old Testament. And God asks, "Is he my darling child?" God is not wondering. It's a declaration, clothed in the gentleness of a question. His people are his "dear son" and even his "darling child."

Is that how you think of God as he looks down at you?

"For as often as I speak against him"—as he has for twenty-nine chapters, rebuking his hard-hearted people—"I do remember him still."

Remember here is not the opposite of forgetting. This is God. He is all-knowing. *Remember* here is covenant language. It means to bear up in his heart. This is remembering not as the alternative to forgetting but as the alternative to *forsaking*.

And then comes the high point of the key verse of the four-chapter center of the book of Jeremiah: "My heart yearns for him."

"My heart." There is another more common Hebrew word for "heart" (*lev*). But here in Jeremiah 31 a less common word is used (*meah*). It refers to the insides of a person, the guts. It is the word used, for example, in 2 Samuel 20:10, when Joab stabs Amasa "in the stomach and spilled his *entrails* to the ground."

God, of course, does not have guts. It is his way of speaking of his innermost reflex, his churning insides, his deepest feelings—in a word, his heart.

And note what the text says his heart does. "My heart *yearns* for him" (Jer. 31:20).

What is it to yearn? It is something different than to bless or to save or even to love. It means to long for someone. But even *longing* doesn't quite capture the strength of the word used here for "yearn." This Hebrew word (*hamah*) at its root means to be restless or disturbed, or even growling or roaring. Do you see what God is telling us about himself, what he is insisting on? His ocean-like affection for his children is not threatened by their messiness, because he is restless to pour out his heart of love on them. Think of a time you were fidgety because you were so eager to do something. Maybe a vacation or special meal. That's a glimpse of what is going on within God as he sees us in our need.

Therefore: "I will surely have mercy on him" (31:20). If you were to translate that literally, it would awkwardly be something like: "Having mercy I will have mercy on him." Sometimes Hebrew says something twice, to drive the point home. The yearning heart of God delivers and redelivers sinners who find themselves unable to rescue themselves. Sinners drowning in their failure and weakness. Sinners who have been sinning for twenty-nine chapters.

Who do you think God is, *in* your sin and your suffering? What kind of person do you believe is hearing you when you pray? How does he feel about you?

His rescue is not cool and calculating. It is a matter of yearning—not yearning for the social media you, the you that you project to everyone around you. Not the you that you wish you were.

Yearning for the real you. The you underneath everything you present to others.

———

The world is starving for a yearning love, a love that remembers instead of forsakes. A love that *must* have us. A love that isn't tied to our loveliness. A love that is bigger than the enveloping darkness we might be walking through even today. Including the darkness of our own doing.

Perhaps you find yourself having a hard time latching onto this idea of a yearning, restless heart. Maybe this idea of God's yearning heart for us just seems too vague, too mushy. Hard to really see.

But what if the vague became concrete? What if the yearning heart of God wasn't just words through the prophet Jeremiah? What if God proved his yearning love by showing up among us here on earth?

"My heart yearns for him." If those words were to get dressed up in human flesh, the way we get dressed up for school or work on a Monday morning—what might those words look like?

It looks like a Galilean carpenter walking around Israel two thousand years ago. It looks like a ministry of restoring dignity to men and women and children through healing and teaching and hugging and forgiving.

And that was just his life. On the cross we see God's yearning heart of love even more deeply. Jesus Christ had always been God's "dear Son" and "darling child," to use the language of Jeremiah 31:20. And on that cross, as Jesus was charged with our guilt, God truly did "speak against him."

And why? So that God could say of us, "I remember him still."

On the cross, we see what God did to satisfy his yearning for us. He went that far. He went all the way.

Repent of your small thoughts of God's heart. Repent and let him love you.

15

Rich in Mercy

But God, being rich in mercy . . .
EPHESIANS 2:4

THE WRITTEN WORKS of Thomas Goodwin (one of our Puritan friends) come down to us in twelve volumes, each volume over five hundred pages. And the first two volumes are given entirely to Ephesians 1 and 2. It's over a thousand pages of sermons on these two chapters of the Bible. And Goodwin slows way down when he comes to Ephesians 2:4, giving several sermons on this single verse:

> But God, being rich in mercy, because of the great love with which he loved us . . .

The broader context says we were dead in our sins (2:1–3). But God reached down and made us alive, delivering us from ourselves.

And why?

Because God is not poor in mercy. He is rich in mercy.

Nowhere else in the Bible is God described as rich in anything. The only thing he is called *rich* in is mercy. What does this mean? It means that God is something other than what we naturally believe him to be. It means the Christian life is a lifelong shedding of our small thoughts on the mercy of God. God's mercy is bigger than we realize.

———

Let's look at the text more closely.

"God, *being* rich in mercy . . ." (Eph. 2:4). *Being*, not *becoming*. Not: he'll be rich in mercy one day. Rather: he is already rich in mercy, for you and me, right now. A statement like that is again taking us into God's very being and nature. "He is the spring of all mercy," says Goodwin. "It is natural to him. It is his nature. When he shows mercy, he does it with his whole heart."[1] This is why he *delights* in mercy

1   Thomas Goodwin, *Exposition of Ephesians 2*, in *The Works of Thomas Goodwin*, 12 vols. (repr., Grand Rapids, MI: Reformation Heritage, 2006), 2:179.

(Mic. 7:18). God is a billionaire in the currency of mercy, and when he gives those riches to us, his own vast fortune is not diminished at all.

How can that be? Because mercy is who he is. If mercy was something he simply had, while his deepest nature was something different, there would be a limit on how much mercy he could produce. But if mercy is his very nature, then for him to pour out mercy is simply for him to be himself. This does not mean he is *only* merciful. He is also perfectly just and holy. He is rightly wrathful against sin and sinners. But wrath is not what he is "rich in."

The text goes on to join God's rich-in-mercy nature with his great love: "God, being rich in mercy, *because of the great love with which he loved us* . . ." (Eph. 2:4).

When the Scripture speaks of "the great love with which he loved us," we must hear what it is saying. Divine love is not just patiently putting up with us. It doesn't stand still; it runs. It is active, not passive. His love is great because it rushes forward all the more when his beloved is threatened, even if threatened as a result of the beloved's own foolishness. We understand this on a human level; an earthly father's love rises up within him when he sees his child accused or afflicted, even if that child really did do something bad. Renewed affection boils up within him.

Perhaps all this talk of mercy and love seems a little abstract or hard to understand. The richness of divine mercy becomes real to us, however, as we see that the river of mercy flowing out of God's heart took shape as a man. When Paul speaks of the saving appearance of Christ, he says, "The grace . . . appeared . . ." (Titus 2:11). The grace and mercy of God became reality in Jesus Christ. Therefore to speak of Christ appearing is to speak of grace appearing. "Christ is nothing but pure grace clothed with our nature," wrote the Puritan pastor Richard Sibbes.[2]

Therefore when we look at the ministry of Christ in the Bible, and especially on the cross, we are seeing what "rich in mercy" (Eph 2:4) looks like—how "rich in mercy" talks, how it lives, how it moves toward sufferers.

———

Consider God's richness in mercy for your own life.

Perhaps, looking at the evidence of your life, you feel as if this mercy of God in Christ has passed you by. Maybe you have been deeply mistreated. Misunderstood. Betrayed by the

2   Richard Sibbes, *The Church's Riches by Christ's Poverty*, in *The Works of Richard Sibbes*, ed. A. B. Grosart, 7 vols. (Edinburgh: Banner of Truth, 1983), 4:518.

one person you should have been able to trust. Abandoned. Perhaps you carry a pain that will never heal till you are dead. *If my life is evidence of the mercy of God in Christ*, you might think, *I'm not impressed.*

To you I say, the evidence of Christ's mercy toward you is not your life. The evidence of his mercy toward you is *his*—mistreated, misunderstood, betrayed, and abandoned life. Eternally. In your place.

If God sent his own Son to walk through the valley of condemnation, rejection, and hell, you can trust him as you walk through your own valleys on your way to heaven.

Perhaps you have difficulty receiving the rich mercy of God in Christ not because of what others have done to you but because of what *you've* done to torpedo your life. Maybe through one big, stupid decision, or maybe through ten thousand little ones. You have squandered his mercy, and you know it.

To you I say, do you know what Jesus does with those who squander his mercy?

He pours out more mercy.

God is rich in mercy. That's the whole point.

Whether we have been sinned against or have sinned ourselves into misery, the Bible says God is not tightfisted with mercy but openhanded, not poor but rich.

That God is rich in mercy means that your regions of deepest shame and regret are not hotels through which divine mercy passes but homes in which divine mercy abides.

It means the things about you that make you cringe most, make him hug hardest.

It means his mercy is not slow and cautious like ours. It is free-flowing and flood-like.

It means our haunting shame is not a problem for him but the very thing he loves most to work with.

It means our sins do not cause his love to take a hit. Our sins cause his love to surge forward all the more.

It means on that day when we stand before him, quietly, unhurriedly, we will weep with relief, shocked at how shallow a view of his mercy-rich heart we had.

16

He Loved Us Then;
He'll Love Us Now

God shows his love for us . . .

ROMANS 5:8

IT IS ONE THING to believe that God has forgiven and put away all our old failures that occurred before we became Christians. That is a wonder of mercy, unspeakably rich! But those were, after all, sins committed while we were still in the dark. We had not been made new creatures, freshly empowered to honor the Lord with our lives.

It's another thing to believe that God continues, just as freely, to put away all our present failures that occur even now that we are Christians.

Perhaps, as believers today, we know God loves us. We really believe that. But if we were to more closely examine how we actually relate to the Father moment by moment, many of us tend to believe it is a love infected with disappointment. We see him looking down on us with fatherly affection but slightly raised eyebrows: "How are they still failing so often after all I have done for them?" we picture him wondering. And we remain discouraged.

Once again, this thinking is a result of projecting our own ability to love onto God. We do not know his heart.

And that is why Romans 5:6–11 is in the Bible.

For while we were still weak, at the right time Christ died for the ungodly. For one will scarcely die for a righteous person—though perhaps for a good person one would dare even to die—but God shows his love for us in that while we were still sinners, Christ died for us. Since, therefore, we have now been justified by his blood, much more shall we be saved by him from the wrath of God. For if while we were enemies we were reconciled to God by the death of his Son, much more, now that we are reconciled, shall we be saved by his life. More than that, we also rejoice in God through our Lord Jesus Christ,

through whom we have now received reconciliation.
(Rom. 5:6–11)

———

In this second paragraph in Romans 5, Paul says roughly the
same thing three times:

While we were still weak, at the right time Christ died for
the ungodly. (5:6)

While we were still sinners, Christ died for us. (5:8)

If *while we were enemies* we were reconciled to God by the
death of his Son . . . (5:10)

To say the same truth backward: Jesus didn't die for us once
we became strong (5:6). He didn't die for us once we started
to overcome our sinfulness (5:8). God did not reconcile us to
himself once we became friendly toward him (5:10).

God didn't hold back, cautious, waiting to see how we
would perform as Christians. He and his Son took the ini-
tiative. On terms of grace and grace alone. In defiance of
what we deserved. When we were running from God as fast
as we could, building our own kingdoms and loving our

own glory—it was then that the prince of heaven bade his adoring angels farewell. It was then that he put himself into the murderous hands of these very rebels. The Son of God stepped down from heaven in a divine plan to rinse muddy sinners clean and hug them into his own heart despite their squirmy attempt to get free and scrub themselves clean on their own. Christ went down into death while we stood by and applauded. We couldn't have cared less. We were weak. Sinners. Enemies.

———

This is the greatest news in the history of the world. But even this is not Paul's main point in Romans 5. He's after something else.

What is Paul concerned with in Romans 5:6–11? Not God's past work, mainly. Paul's deepest burden is our present safety, given that past work.

He talks about Christ's past work to drive home this point: if God did that back then, when you were so lost and had zero interest in him, then what are you worried about now?

The central burden of verses 6 through 11 is captured in the "since" of verse 9: "*Since*, therefore, we have now been justified by his blood,"—and now we hear Paul's driving concern— "much more shall we be saved by him from the wrath of God."

Verse 10 drives the point even further home: "For if while we were enemies we were reconciled to God by the death of his Son"—and here's the point again—"much more, now that we are reconciled, shall we be saved by his life."

Paul is saying that God doesn't save you, only to abandon you when you fail. He looks after us right into heaven. Conversion isn't a fresh start. Conversion means it is now certain and safe that we will make it to heaven. We were enemies when God came to us and justified us; how much more will God care for us now that we are his friends—indeed, his children? As the English theologian John Flavel put it, "As God did not at first choose you because you were high, he will not now forsake you because you are low."[1]

How easily we who have been united to Christ wonder what God thinks of us in our failures now. The logic of Romans 5 is: Through his Son he drew near to us when we hated him. Will he remain distant now that we hope we can please him?

He eagerly suffered for us when we were failing, as orphans. Will he cross his arms over our failures now that we are his adopted children?

---

1 John Flavel, *Keeping the Heart: How to Maintain Your Love for God* (Fearn, UK: Christian Focus, 2012), 43.

His heart was gentle and lowly toward us when we were lost. Will his heart be anything different toward us now that we are found?

———

"*While we were still....*" He loved us in our mess then. He'll love us in our mess now. The very fact that our sin troubles us is a reflection of our adoption. A cold heart would not be bothered. We are not who we were.

When you sin, do a thorough job of repenting. Re-hate sin all over again. Give yourself over to God once more. But also reject the devil's whisper that God's tender heart for you has grown a little colder.

If you are in Christ, your disobedience does not threaten your place in the love of God. The hardest part has been accomplished. In Christ's death, God has secured your eternal happiness. And he did that while you were an orphan. Nothing can now un-child you. Not even you.

If you are united to Christ, you are as good as in heaven already.

17

To the End

Having loved his own who were in the
world, he loved them to the end.

JOHN 13:1

WHAT WE ARE SEEING in this book is that the heart of Christ for sinners and sufferers does not flash with tenderness occasionally or temporarily, sputtering out over time. Gentleness and lowliness of heart is who Christ always is. He is gentle and lowly steadily, consistently, everlastingly, when all loveliness in us has withered.

How do we know?

We know because of John 13:1:

Now before the Feast of the Passover, when Jesus knew that his hour had come to depart out of this world to the

Father, having loved his own who were in the world, he loved them to the end.

Jesus knows that this is the beginning of the end for him. He is entering the final chapter and deepest valley of his earthly ministry. He "knew that his hour had come to depart out of this world."

John then pauses in a moment of moving reflection and looks back over Jesus's ministry and forward to the final week. Looking back, John says, Jesus had "loved his own who were in the world." Looking forward, "he loved them to the end."

———

Jesus's ministry to this point has been utterly demanding. He has been tired and hungry. He has been mocked and accused by the religious leaders. And he has been misunderstood and mistreated by his own family.

But what is all this compared to what now lay before him at the cross? What is a cold rain compared to drowning?

For consider exactly what was about to happen. His worst nightmare was about to wash over him. Hell itself—the horror of condemnation and darkness and death—was opening its jaws.

What *happened* at the cross, for those of us who are in Christ?

After all, God punished Jesus not for the sin of just one person but many. What must it mean when Isaiah says of the servant that

the LORD has laid on him
the iniquity *of us all* (Isa. 53:6)?

What must it have been for the sum total of all the wrath that is deserved by all of God's people to come crashing down on a single soul?

Who could possibly bear up beneath it? Who would not cry out and shut down?

What must the cross have been like for Jesus? He had been receiving the love of God as his oxygen, without a single moment of interruption by sin—and suddenly the unspeakable weight of all our sins came sweeping down upon him. Who could possibly survive that?

———

But why would he go through with it? Why would he step down into the horror of hellish condemnation when he was the one person who didn't deserve it?

The text tells us. "Having *loved* his own . . . he *loved* them to the end" (John 13:1). Jesus came to the cliff of the cross and didn't change his mind. He walked over the edge.

He does not love like we do.

We love until we are betrayed. Jesus continued to the cross despite betrayal. We love until we are forsaken. Jesus loved through forsakenness.

We love up to a limit. Jesus loves to the end.

As John Bunyan puts it, "Christ is love. He may as well cease to be, as cease to love."[1]

When the apostle John tells us that Jesus loved his own to the end, John is pulling back the veil to allow us to peer into the depths of who Jesus is. His heart for his own is not like an arrow, shot quickly but soon falling to the ground; or a runner, quick out of the gate, soon slowing and getting tired. His heart is an avalanche, gathering momentum with time; a wildfire, growing in intensity as it spreads.

This is not who Christ is for everyone. The text says it is "his own" whom he loves to the end. "His own" is a phrase used throughout John's writings to refer to Christ's true disciples, the children of God. To those who are not

---

1 John Bunyan, *The Saints' Knowledge of Christ's Love*, in *The Works of John Bunyan*, ed. George Offor, 3 vols. (repr., Edinburgh: Banner of Truth, 1991), 2:17.

his own, Jesus is a fearful judge, one whose wrath cannot be avoided.

But for his own, Jesus himself endured that punishment. He set his heart on his own. They are his. "There is not the meanest, the weakest, the poorest believer on the earth," wrote the great theologian John Owen, "but Christ prizes him more than all the world."[2]

Jesus Christ loved his own all the way through death itself. What must that mean for you? It means that your future is secure. If you are his, heaven and relief is coming, for you cannot be made un-his. He made you his own, and you can't squirm out of his grasp.

Jesus endured hell so you could have heaven. He lost God's love so you could have it.

Jesus Christ loved you when you first fell into his arms. He will love you to the end.

2 John Owen, *Communion with God* (Fearn, UK: Christian Heritage, 2012), 218.

18

Buried in His Heart
Forevermore

. . . so that in the coming ages he might
show the immeasurable riches of his
grace in kindness toward us.

EPHESIANS 2:7

WHAT'S THE MEANING OF EVERYTHING? What's the final
purpose or goal for our small, ordinary lives?

Earlier in our study of Christ's heart, we considered the
phrase "rich in mercy" in Ephesians 2:4. At the end of the
long sentence that begins in verse 4, Paul gives us (in verse 7)
the ultimate reason for our salvation. The whole sentence
goes like this:

But God, being rich in mercy, because of the great love with which he loved us, even when we were dead in our trespasses, made us alive together with Christ—by grace you have been saved—and raised us up with him and seated us with him in the heavenly places in Christ Jesus, so that in the coming ages he might show the immeasurable riches of his grace in kindness toward us in Christ Jesus. (Eph. 2:4–7)

What is the point of unending eternal life in the new heavens and the new earth? It is that God "might show the immeasurable riches of his grace in kindness toward us in Christ Jesus."

Here we are. Just ordinary people, anxiously making our way through life, sinning and suffering, wandering and returning, regretting and despairing. Often drifting away from a heart sense of what we will enjoy forever if we are in Christ. Life is hard.

Does a text like Ephesians 2:7 connect with our actual lives? *Or is it just for the theologians to write about?*

———

As we close our study of the heart of Christ, I would like to linger over Ephesians 2:7. Let's consider exactly what we are being liberated into by this short text:

So that in the coming ages he might show the immeasurable riches of his grace in kindness toward us in Christ Jesus.

What does that mean, for those in Christ?

It means that one day God is going to walk us through the wardrobe into Narnia. There we will stand, fearless and free, paralyzed with joy, wonder, astonishment, and relief.

It means that as we stand there, we will never be scolded for the sins of this life. The very point of heaven and eternity is to enjoy his "grace in kindness." And if the point of heaven is to show the riches of his grace, then we are safe, because the one thing we fear will keep us out—our sin—can only heighten our wonder at God's grace.

It means that our sinfulness now is not an obstacle to enjoying heaven. Our sinfulness is the key ingredient to enjoying heaven. Whatever mess we have made of our lives—*that* is part of our final glory and calm and radiance. That thing we've done that sent our life into meltdown—that is where God in Christ becomes more real than ever in this life and more wonderful to us in the next.

If his grace in kindness is "immeasurable" (without any limit), then our failures can never weaken his grace. Our moments of feeling utterly overwhelmed by life are where God's heart lives. Our deepest places of failure and regret are where his heart is drawn most strongly.

If his grace in kindness is "immeasurable *riches*" (2:7)—as opposed to measurable, middle-class grace—then our sins can never exhaust his heart. On the contrary, the more weakness and failure, the more his heart goes out to us.

Ephesians 2:7 doesn't just say the "immeasurable riches of his grace" but "the immeasurable riches of his grace *in kindness*." The Greek word for *kindness* means "a desire to do what is in your power to prevent discomfort in another." It's the same word used in Matthew 11:30 where Jesus says "my yoke is *easy*." His yoke is kind.

His grace in kindness is "toward us in Christ Jesus" (Eph. 2:7). Do you realize what is true of you if you are *in Christ*? Those united to him are promised that all the haunted brokenness that infects everything—every relationship, every conversation, every family, every class, every job, every vacation—everything—will one day be rewound and reversed. The more darkness and pain we experience in this life, the more brightness and relief in the next. As a character says in C. S. Lewis's 1945 book *The Great Divorce*, reflecting biblical teaching:

> That is what mortals misunderstand. They say of some temporal suffering, "No future bliss can make up for it,"

not knowing that Heaven, once attained, will work back-wards and turn even that agony into a glory.[1]

If you are in Christ, you have been made eternally invincible. Even now.

———

Ephesians 2:7 is telling you that your death is not an end but a beginning. Not a wall, but a door. Not an exit, but an entrance.

The point of all human history and eternity itself is to show what cannot be fully shown. To demonstrate what cannot be fully demonstrated. In the coming age we will descend ever deeper into God's grace in kindness, into his very heart, and the more we understand of it, the more we will see it to be beyond understanding. It is immeasurable.

For those not in Christ, this life is the best it will ever get. For those in Christ, this life is the worst it will ever get.

1 C. S. Lewis, *The Great Divorce* (New York: HarperCollins, 2001), 69.

Conclusion

The Point of This Whole Book

This is a book about the heart of Christ and of God. But what are we to do with this information?

The main answer is, *nothing*. To ask, "Now how do I apply this to my life?" would miss the point of this study. If someone from the South Pole wins a vacation to the Bahamas, he doesn't arrive in his hotel room, step out onto the balcony, and wonder how to apply that to his life. He just enjoys it. He just basks.

So there is just one thing, really, for us to do. Jesus says it in Matthew 11:28:

"Come to me."

Why do we not do this? Thomas Goodwin tells us. It's the whole point of our study of Jesus. He says that the reason people do not go to Jesus is that "they know not Christ's mind and heart." Goodwin goes on: "The truth is, he is more glad of us than we can be of him." In other words, Jesus is more eager for you to go to him than you can ever be. So Goodwin concludes: "O therefore come in unto him. If you knew his heart, you would."[1]

Go to him. All that means is, open yourself up to him. Talk to him. Allow yourself to *feel* forgiven. Let him love you.

The Christian life boils down to two steps:

1. Go to Jesus.
2. See Step 1.

Whatever is crumbling all around you in your life, wherever you feel stuck, this remains: his heart for you, the real you, is gentle and lowly. So go to him. That place in your life where you feel most defeated, he is there. He lives there, right there, and his heart for you, now and forever, is gentle and lowly.

Your anguish is his home. Go to him.

"If you knew his heart, you would."

---

1 Thomas Goodwin, *Encouragements to Faith*, in *The Works of Thomas Goodwin*, 12 vols. (repr., Grand Rapids, MI: Reformation Heritage, 2006), 4:223–24.

Acknowledgments

THIS CONCISE EDITION stands on the shoulders of the previous book, *Gentle and Lowly*, and therefore I reiterate my deep appreciation to those who helped make that initial version appear: Stacey, Eric, Gavin, Dad, Drew, Mike, Art, Lane, Justin, Dave, and Lydia.

Thank you, Josh Dennis and Don Jones, for approaching me with the idea for this book, and for being such cheerful and encouraging teammates in it.

I thank Naperville Presbyterian Church for the six-week writing leave in summer 2023 that gave me the concentrated and extended season of time to focus on creating the present version. What a journey into the love of the Greatheart we find ourselves enjoying together, NPC!

This new version received the excellent editorial care of Laura Yiesla, for which I am most grateful. Thank you, Laura.

I dedicate this book to my five wonderful kids: Zach, Nate, Jeremiah, Chloe, and Ben. I wrote it for you and your friends. Thanks for talking with me about it and thanks for encouraging me. I love you with all my heart. May you know, more and more, his heart.

General Index

Scripture Index